P9-CQF-489

RALPH NADER

Other titles in the
PEOPLE WHO MADE A DIFFERENCE
series include

Louis Braille
Marie Curie
Father Damien
Mahatma Gandhi
Bob Geldof
Martin Luther King, Jr.
Florence Nightingale
Albert Schweitzer
Mother Teresa
Sojourner Truth
Desmond Tutu

A Gareth Stevens Children's Books edition

Edited, designed, and produced by
Gareth Stevens Children's Books
1555 North RiverCenter Drive, Suite 201
Milwaukee, Wisconsin 53212, USA

First published in the United States and Canada in 1991 by
Gareth Stevens, Inc. This edition is abridged from *Ralph
Nader: Crusader for safe consumer products and lawyer for the
public interest*, published in 1990 by Gareth Stevens, Inc., and
written by Kelli Peduzzi. Text, end matter, and format
copyright © 1991 by Gareth Stevens, Inc.

Library of Congress Cataloging-in-Publication Data

Tolan, Mary M., 195?-
    Ralph Nader / Mary M. Tolan's adaptation of the book by
Kelli Peduzzi. — North American ed.
      p. cm. — (People who made a difference)
    Includes bibliographical references and index.
    Summary: A biography of the consumer advocate who
devotes his life to crusading for citizens' rights, such as safer
cars, cleaner food, and truthful advertising.
    ISBN 0-8368-0455-4
    1. Nader, Ralph—Juvenile literature. 2. Consumer affairs
directors—United States—Biography—Juvenile
literature. 3. Lobbyists—United States—Biography—
Juvenile literature. 4. Consumer protection—United States
—Juvenile literature. [1. Nader, Ralph. 2. Consumer affairs
directors. 3. Lobbyists. 4. Consumer protection.] I. Peduzzi,
Kelli. Ralph Nader. II. Title. III. Series.
HC110.C63N328   1990   343.73'07092—dc20
[B]   [347.3037092] [B]   [92]   90-9924

For a free color catalog describing
Gareth Stevens' list of high-quality
children's books, call

1-800-341-3569 (USA) or
1-800-461-9120 (Canada)

PICTURE CREDITS
The Bettmann Archive — 11 (upper
right), 27, 32, 34; Cindy Lewis Photo-
graphy — 5; map by Sharon Burris,
© Gareth Stevens, Inc., 1989 — 8; © Kara-
lee Helminak, 1989 — 52; Lake County
(Illinois) Museum, Curt Teich Archives
— 7, 10, 13, 24, 35, 48; Photo courtesy of
Milwaukee County Historical Society —
29; Tom Redman — cover illustration;
Torrington Register Citizen — 54, 55;
UPI/Bettmann Newsphotos — 4, 6, 14,
16, 17, 18, 19, 21, 23, 25, 31, 33, 37 (both),
43, 51, 59; U.S. Department of
Agriculture — 11 (lower left), 19, 22, 47;
Wide World Photos — 40.

The reproduction rights to all
photographs and illustrations in this book
are controlled by the individuals or
institutions credited above and may not be
reproduced without their permission.

Series conceived by Helen Exley
Series editor: Amy Bauman
Editor: Tom Barnett
Editorial assistants: Scott Enk, Diane Laska, John D. Rateliff
Cover design: Kate Kriege
Layout: Kristi Ludwig
Picture research: Daniel Helminak

Printed in the United States of America

1 2 3 4 5 6 7 8 9 95 94 93 92 91

*Crusader
for safe
consumer
products*

RALPH NADER

Mary Tolan

Kelli Peduzzi

Gareth Stevens Children's Books
MILWAUKEE

Unsafe at any speed

"For over half a century the automobile has brought death, injury, [and] . . . sorrow . . . to millions of people." So began a book published in 1965 called *Unsafe at Any Speed.* The book was written by a young, unknown lawyer from New York named Ralph Nader.

Nader's book told the truth about many highway traffic deaths. In it, he said automobile makers were designing and making unsafe cars. He claimed that while the cars might look nice, most increased passengers' chances for injury.

Nader also said that the large car companies did not care about the people who bought their cars. He said they knew how to make their cars safer, but they cared more about making lots of money than they did about making safe cars. And he decided to tell Americans about this problem.

The book was very popular. Within a year, it was on the best-seller list. During the next three decades, this man continued to tell Americans how government and business policies were affecting their lives.

Opposite: Ralph Nader first spoke to a U.S. Senate committee about unsafe cars in 1966. He was angry about the design and production of some cars, which he felt were unsafe. Nader said that people had a right to know about a car's safety record.

The Corvair was the subject of Ralph Nader's investigation.

5

The frightening Corvair

Nader had carefully studied the car industry. From his work, he made some frightening discoveries. He claimed that one car, the Corvair, was the most dangerous of all. He said that it caused more deaths on the highway than any other automobile. The problem was that its maker, General Motors (GM), wanted the Corvair to look sporty, since that would help it sell fast. But they did not worry about its safety features.

The Corvair first appeared in 1959. In the next few years, 106 owners of that model took General Motors to court. The car was not stable, owners claimed. It would spin or roll over at the slightest bump in the road.

Careless and greedy

Ralph Nader was the first person to blame a car's design for causing injuries and death. He became curious about this idea in the late 1950s. At that time, he had been reading about how many people in the United States died in car accidents every year. Surely all the accidents couldn't be due to bad driving, he thought. There must be something wrong with automobile design. So he began his research.

Nader claimed that automakers were purposely making cars without enough safety features. This practice, he added,

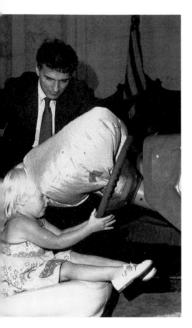

Nader watches as an "air bag" protects a little girl during a safety test. Nader asked Congress to pass a law requiring air bags in all new cars. But carmakers fought against this idea, and it never became a law.

"That's the sixth [accident] this month. I tell you, Dan, there's something wrong with the Corvair. I don't know [what's causing it], but [those] cars . . . should never have been in accidents."

A California highway patrolman to his partner, quoted in Richard Curtis' Ralph Nader's Crusade

---

meant more accidents. So he suggested that all cars have seat belts, shock-absorbing bumpers, and padded dashboards. These would help protect people from injuries.

He also argued that the number of car accidents was creating huge profits for business. People were paying a lot of money to doctors, lawyers, insurance agents, car mechanics, and funeral directors. And this was all because of car accidents that didn't need to happen.

Nader backed up his arguments with facts. There was no doubt about it. General Motors, he concluded, was selling a dangerous car. The company did not care about consumer safety. Its lack of concern was causing injury and death. But nobody was demanding answers from GM.

Nader was furious. GM was spending very little money to study auto safety. Yet it was making billions of dollars

Driver safety warnings like this one from 1960 warned drivers to be careful when driving. But the people who had them made did not see the dangers in the cars themselves.

BE AWARE
BE ALERT

THINK ONLY OF DRIVING !
In Case of EMERGENCY — Read REVERSE Side

BE COURTEOUS
BE SAFE

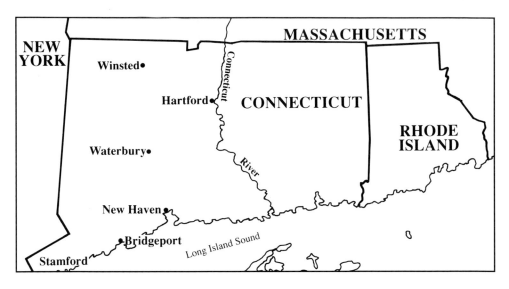

New York — Winsted • — Hartford • — MASSACHUSETTS — Connecticut River — CONNECTICUT — RHODE ISLAND — Waterbury • — New Haven • — Bridgeport • — Stamford — Long Island Sound

Winsted, Connecticut, is a small town in the northwestern part of the state.

selling its cars. So GM was not just careless. It was greedy, too.

Of course, people at General Motors' headquarters in Detroit, Michigan, heard about Nader's book. They worried that the public would listen to what Ralph Nader was saying. If the public did listen, GM could lose a lot of money. They began to wonder about this young lawyer named Ralph Nader.

Nathra Nader

"My father used to tell me what lawyers could do compared to what they did do. I learned that the legal profession was [a perfect] spot from which to try to improve society."

Ralph Nader, quoted in Richard Curtis' Ralph Nader's Crusade

Ralph Nader was born on February 27, 1934, to Nathra and Rose Nader. He was the youngest of their four children. The Naders had two boys and two girls: Shafik, Claire, Laura, and Ralph.

Ralph's parents had come to the United States from Lebanon in 1912. After a few years in New York, the family settled in Winsted, Connecticut.

Nathra, Ralph's father, worked hard. He opened a restaurant called the Highland Arms across the street from their home. With the food he served, he also handed out his opinions. He had a lot to say about everything.

Nathra Nader also attended many town meetings. He would demand information about how tax money was being spent. He told people how the town should deal with its problems. Ralph often went with his father to the meetings. He was fascinated by what went on at them.

Nathra had advice for his children, too. He often told them to rely on themselves. "It is the individual's duty to speak out," he would say. "What is the value of freedom if people don't use it?"

Nathra had great respect for freedom — especially for freedom of speech. He passed this respect for freedom on to his children, along with a great concern for other people.

Rose Nader

Ralph's mother, Rose, worked at home while her children were growing up. This way, she felt she could support and encourage them. She was a kind mother. She taught her children that it was important to care about other people.

Rose was also a strict parent. One of her beliefs was that the children should

"We couldn't just complain. If we said we didn't like something, we were told to do something about it."
Laura Nader, quoted in Hays Gorey's Nader and the Power of Everyman

"I taught Ralph to be human, to think of others before he thought of himself. This, I think, is the essence of his appeal."
Rose Nader, quoted in Robert Buckhorn's Nader, the People's Lawyer

"It was not appropriate to quit. You had to argue for the position you had, but the wonderful thing was that nothing said, no matter how heated, was allowed to disturb the family relationship. But if you couldn't stand the truth, you didn't ask Dad."
Claire Nader, quoted in Robert Buckhorn's Nader, the People's Lawyer

Nader went to college at Princeton University from 1951 to 1955. Here, the ivy-covered walls of Blair Tower loom like a medieval castle over the campus.

learn something from everything they did. For example, the children would sometimes ask to go to a movie. Rose would find out all she could about the movie before she would agree. She had to be sure that the children would learn something from it.

She also raised her children to be independent. One specific family tradition helped the Nader children practice this. Every night, the family had dinner together. At the table, Nathra would encourage discussions. He began each meal by asking a question about a problem. During the meal, the family would try to solve it. Each child was encouraged to talk and to back up his or her opinions. The talk often lasted long after dessert and into the night.

The serious boy

At an early age, Ralph became fascinated with the law. He often visited the courthouse, listening to lawyers argue cases in front of the jury. His parents didn't mind this. In fact, they encouraged his curiosity.

Ralph's father told him that a lawyer could make lasting changes in the world. Ralph knew he wanted to make the world a better place. So he also knew very early that he wanted to be a lawyer.

Even when most of his friends were outside playing ball, Ralph could be found inside the courthouse or library. Many of his teachers remember him as a serious, hard-working boy.

On to the university

In the fall of 1951, Ralph entered Princeton University in New Jersey. His parents had carefully saved money for his college education, just as they had for his brother and sisters.

Once at Princeton, Ralph decided that most of the other students were more interested in having fun than in learning. He thought they cared too much about what they wore, what they drove, and with whom they were seen.

Many people at Princeton thought Ralph was shy. He made few friends. But those friends knew he wasn't shy. He just didn't talk about the things that other college students talked about, such as

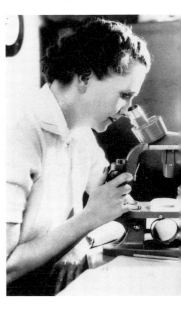

In 1962, Rachel Carson wrote Silent Spring. *This book showed the dangers of using certain pesticides — chemicals used to kill insects and other pests.*

Ralph Nader says that pollution is a consumer issue because people cannot avoid drinking, eating, and breathing industrial pollution and poisonous wastes. He insists that industry pay its share of the cost of cleaning up the environment it has poisoned.

11

sports or dating. But his friends knew that if he started talking about politics or social issues, he could go on forever.

The beginning of a career

Ralph noticed that birds were dying on Princeton's campus. He knew that the trees were being sprayed with a chemical for killing insects, called DDT. Nader was worried. If the DDT was killing birds, what was it doing to people?

Nader wrote a letter to the school newspaper and explained the situation. He said that the pesticide should not be used on the campus. The paper refused to print his letter. Ralph was shocked. He couldn't believe that people could ignore such dangers in the environment.

Years later, writer Rachel Carson wrote a book called *Silent Spring*. In it, she proved the dangers of DDT. After her book was published in 1962, the government banned DDT.

Disappointed with school

Ralph graduated from Princeton with honors. In the fall of 1955, he eagerly entered Harvard Law School. He believed that the law was meant to be used to correct social wrongs. He wanted to become a public-interest lawyer. A public-interest lawyer works for causes that help individual citizens and protect their rights.

But Nader was again disappointed. Almost all of the law courses were about business and corporate law. These classes taught students how to use the law to serve rich and powerful businesses. Many of his classmates seemed to want to be lawyers only to get rich by serving powerful businesses. Nader was disgusted. This was not what he had expected. He promised himself that he would become a public-interest lawyer despite the school's training.

As Ralph said years later, "they were training us to be experts in servicing big businesses. In the meantime, the problems of the cities were building up, racial problems were building up, environmental problems were building up. . . . And we weren't even exposed to these as challenges to our profession."

Hitchhiking to a cause

What Nader couldn't learn at Harvard, he taught himself. He read the law on his own. He was very interested in laws that had to do with social problems — problems that affected many people.

And when he wasn't reading law, Nader began to hitchhike around the country. He wanted to see as much of it as he could. It was during his hitchhiking days that he became interested in highway safety. On the road, he saw many terrible accidents and

The truckers Nader met when crossing the country saw many warnings such as this. Not until Nader's work roused them to anger, however, did the public decide that being a good driver wasn't enough. They wanted well-constructed vehicles.

many badly injured people. He began to talk about safety with the truck drivers who gave him rides. Nader learned that many of them had been injured because their trucks were badly built.

Making a name for himself

Nader wrote an article about his experiences on the road. It was called "American Cars: Designed for Death." The *Harvard Law School Record* published it on December 11, 1958. A few months later, he published another article, "The Safe Car You Can't Buy." It came out in a magazine, the *Nation*. Many people from across the country asked him for copies of the article. They wanted to hear what he had to say about how the automobile industry was making cars that weren't as safe as they could be. He was becoming an advocate — someone who speaks in favor of an issue or cause.

Daniel Patrick Moynihan was assistant secretary of labor in 1965. He was Ralph Nader's first important friend in Washington, D.C. He invited Nader to come and work for him on auto safety investigations.

From Connecticut to Washington, D.C.

Nader worked as a cook in the Army Reserve for six months after graduation. After that, he returned to Connecticut and opened a small law office.

People who were having problems with government agencies began asking Nader for help. They felt he was on their side and could fight for them.

14

Nader tried to establish a system that would help people handle problems like these. In this system, one person would represent citizens and handle their problems with the government. Nader helped write a bill to create such a system and sent it to Connecticut's state government in 1963. It didn't pass. But this was one of Nader's earliest efforts to help ordinary people.

In 1964, Daniel Patrick Moynihan offered Nader a job in Washington, D.C. Moynihan was assistant secretary of labor under President Lyndon B. Johnson. Nader and Moynihan had known each other since Nader was at Harvard. Nader read Moynihan's writings on tire safety and they had been writing to each other ever since then.

Nader was not happy working in Connecticut. He felt he wasn't dealing with any big issues that would bring about change. Moynihan asked Nader to come to Washington and work with his agency on highway safety. Nader went.

But his work with Moynihan was not enough, either. He left his job with Moynihan to research the problem of dangerous car design.

It was during this period that he researched the book *Unsafe at Any Speed*. The book was published in 1965. Sales of the Corvair then dropped 93 percent. General Motors officials were shocked.

"He seems to be a bit of a nut or some kind of a screwball."
Richard Danner, attorney for General Motors, quoted in Robert Buckhorn's Nader, the People's Lawyer

"The key to living an exciting professional life is to live a dull personal life. Why is it supposed to be so much more pleasurable to watch a movie or a football game or listen to music than to protect the consumer interest?"
Ralph Nader, quoted in Hays Gorey's Nader and the Power of Everyman

"He's an original. There's no one like him anywhere in the world. And I mean that in the finest sense. No single individual has done more to dramatize the interests and needs of the ordinary citizen."
Senator Abraham Ribicoff, quoted in Hays Gorey's Nader and the Power of Everyman

GM's secret investigation

The officials at GM decided to do something about Ralph Nader. They hired private detectives to watch him. The detectives were told to find out something about Nader that GM could use against him. Then maybe people would stop listening to what he was saying about the auto industry.

But the detectives could not find anything shocking about Nader to tell the GM officials. Nader didn't drink, smoke, or gamble. They said Nader didn't even seem to date.

By now, the GM officials had spent thousands of dollars spying on Nader. Now, finally, they gave up. They could find nothing to make Nader look bad.

Brought to justice

But it was too late. Senate security guards had seen detectives following Nader into the U.S. Capitol building. He had gone there to testify on auto safety.

The guards ordered the men to leave. But later, the guards told Senator Abraham Ribicoff what they had seen. Ribicoff was leading a U.S. Senate investigation into highway safety. Nader was one of this investigation's witnesses. Ribicoff suspected that the men had been trying to harass — to frighten — Nader. He knew that harassing a witness is a crime. So he told Nader.

Senator Abraham Ribicoff led a congressional investigation on highway safety in 1966. He alerted Nader when he learned that Nader was being followed by detectives in the nation's Capitol.

"Ralph Nader is perhaps the single most effective antagonist of American business."

Associate Justice
Lewis F. Powell, Jr.,
U.S. Supreme Court, quoted
in Hays Gorey's Nader and
the Power of Everyman

In March 1966, a *New York Times* story accused GM of spying on Nader. Many people had never heard of Ralph Nader. But people had certainly heard of General Motors. The idea of a giant corporation spying on a private citizen did not make GM look good. The company denied that there had ever been any investigation.

That made Nader mad. He decided to do something about it. With Ribicoff's help, Nader brought the case to Ribicoff's Senate committee.

The committee held meetings, or hearings, at which people were questioned about auto safety. James Roche, the chairman of General Motors, was one of the people questioned.

This was Nader's chance. He showed proof that GM had been spying on him. Roche was embarrassed. He said he hadn't known anything about the spying. But he could not deny the facts. He apologized publicly to Nader.

James Roche, then chairman of General Motors, insisted that he did not know of GM's spying activities. Later, he publicly apologized to Nader.

"True, he does what he does out of a compulsion. But he just loves it. He is having a ball."
Reuben Robertson, attorney at the Center for the Study of Responsive Law, quoted in Robert Buckhorn's Nader, the People's Lawyer

An awakening

Newspapers across the country ran stories about the event. All of America was shocked. People suddenly realized that this man, Ralph Nader, had been working to make their lives better. They began to see him as a symbol of honesty and the power of the ordinary person to improve society.

"GM can be caught lying and making defective cars, but if Nader is caught just once on something big, he will be destroyed."
A Washington lobbyist, quoted in Robert Buckhorn's Nader, the People's Lawyer

But Ralph Nader was just getting started. He sued GM for what they had done to him. He felt that he should get $26 million from the company. But the case never went to trial because Nader and the company agreed on a payment of $425,000. GM officials probably thought that the money would keep Nader quiet. Then the whole mess could be forgotten.

But they were very wrong. Nader was not going to give up the fight now. He had seen how he, a private citizen, could make a huge corporation tremble.

How Nader spent $425,000

The money from GM did not quiet Ralph Nader at all. In fact, it gave him a chance to begin the career he had always dreamed of. Since his Harvard days, Nader had wanted to start a public-

Ralph Nader appears in a familiar pose behind a forest of microphones at a meeting of Public Citizen. This is one of nineteen consumer groups that he started.

18

interest law office. He imagined an organization that would work to protect public instead of business interests.

The $425,000 was just what Nader needed to turn his dream into reality. With it, he would hire experts in engineering, medicine, chemistry, and biology to lead investigations in their fields. And Ralph would be the unpaid chairman of the board. Money that he made from giving speeches, profits from the sale of his books, and money from grants and foundations would help fund these investigations.

When people heard what Nader was doing, money began to roll in — from rumpled dollar bills to a $100,000 check. It was clear to Nader that people were excited about his dream.

"Working for Ralph gives you a feeling of power. You walk into someone's office, and you can almost see [that person] sweat. It isn't a nice feeling, though. It's rather frightening. Many corporations are running scared, and the officer you talk to knows that not only his job but also the stock of the company, and maybe the company itself, is on the line."

A Nader's Raider, quoted in Richard Curtis' Ralph Nader's Crusade

Power to the people

The law firm would be based on Nader's beliefs about the way businesses and government should treat people. Most important, it would encourage people to speak out and fight to change unfair and harmful policies.

Nader wanted people to see how important it was to be alert, informed consumers. He encouraged workers to "blow the whistle" on employers who created dangerous working conditions.

Nader said that people should be aware of safety or health hazards at

A beautiful park in Little Rock, Arkansas, is marked with this health warning. Nader urges people to fight pollution. Otherwise, he fears, pollution will lead to more problems like this.

work. He said that people should report such dangers to their employers. If those in charge didn't end the danger, then the employees should tell someone outside the business and demand changes.

Nader's law firm would be a place for people to turn if they felt no one was paying attention to their complaints. The firms lawyers would share Ralph Nader's disgust for the way powerful institutions cheated the public. And it would encourage citizens to know the facts about anything directly affecting their lives.

The Center

In May 1969, Nader opened the Center for the Study of Responsive Law (CSRL), known as the Center. He hired six eager young lawyers to start investigating several serious problems.

The headquarters of this nonprofit firm was an old red brick mansion in Washington, D.C. There were no signs outside the building to let people know about the Center. The lawn wasn't mowed. Inside were piles of old newspapers, cardboard boxes full of files, and worn furniture. Two telephone switchboards were always busy.

Upstairs in the offices, padlocks were put on the doors to protect the valuable information inside. Much of what was in the files could be used against big

"If they're willing to work for what I pay them, then they're genuinely interested. If they're not, then there are other places they can go."
Ralph Nader, about offering Raiders low pay, quoted in Richard Curtis' Ralph Nader's Crusade

businesses and even government agencies. There was almost no heat in the winter. Ralph's office had piles of books on the floor and a picture of Thomas Jefferson pinned to the wall.

In 1971, this building was torn down to make way for Washington's new subway system. The new Center headquarters was modern and had heat, but it still looked messy inside.

Ralph Nader talks to students at the Illinois Public Action Council in Champaign, Illinois, in 1984. Nader wants more Americans to become what he calls public citizens, people who become involved in local issues in order to bring about change.

Nader's Raiders

Even though Ralph didn't have much respect for his former universities, Princeton and Harvard, most of the Center's early members had attended those schools.

Nader made it clear from the start that his staff would not be paid much. His young "Raiders," as the press called them, would make only about half of

"The image [of this being glamorous work] is so far off! . . . It's working long hard hours, reading day after day what is boring — trivia, hearings, memos, letters, scholarly treatises. It's just hard, tedious work."
A Nader's Raider, quoted in Richard Curtis' Ralph Nader's Crusade

what they could earn in a big business law firm. And they would work very long hours. Their job would definitely not be easy. They would have to do work on their own and find projects they wanted to investigate. "I'm looking for self-starters," Nader said.

Not an easy job

The Raiders would have to read lots and lots of documents. Each document could contain information that might be used in their battles.

They would also have to do hundreds of interviews for each project. They often had to find ways to talk to people who didn't want to be interviewed.

In 1970, sights like this reminded Nader that public action is meant to reach not just corporations and government bodies, but also private citizens who litter the environment in this way.

The job sounded very hard and filled with thrills and glamour. Demanding, yes. But full of thrills and glamour? Not always. Some of the Raiders even resented that nickname. They said the long hours in the library and office made the job seem more like that of a student than a raider.

A tough staff

In the years since 1969, Nader's staff has investigated thousands of problems. Some of the investigations were about poorly made products, others on bad business practices. If there were no safety standards for a product, the Raiders exposed its poor quality or

Senator Warren G. Magnuson displays burned children's pajamas at the Senate hearings on the Flammable Fabrics Amendments of 1967. Because of such hearings, the law now requires all children's pajamas to be fire-resistant.

23

dangerous construction. If the products actually harmed consumers, Nader and his staff demanded that the businesses that made the products take the blame as well as do something to remedy the problem. And if companies broke laws, they exposed that too.

No industry was beyond the Raiders' examination. Nor were government agencies. Nader wanted to make sure that these agencies were doing a decent job of enforcing health and safety standards. Through the work of the Center, Nader was protecting the trusting public from waste, fraud, exploitation, and danger.

His outrage was contagious. And it surfaced quickly when he found lying and greed.

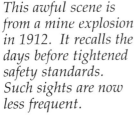

This awful scene is from a mine explosion in 1912. It recalls the days before tightened safety standards. Such sights are now less frequent.

The consumer revolution

In the 1960s, Nader and his Raiders launched the consumer revolution. Citizens all over the country were claiming their rights as consumers. And America's business leaders watched nervously. People began to demand better-made cars, more wholesome food, prescription drugs that were in safety bottles, safer toys and clothes, and cleaner air.

And they listened to this man, Ralph Nader, who told them they could make a difference. They didn't accept the way things were. They could stand up and refuse to be victims of such things as bad automobile design or poisonous air pollution. Citizens learned to raise their voices and demand answers.

Nader and young women from Miss Porter's School discuss their campaign to expose poor conditions in nursing homes for the elderly. "This is a case of the very young reaching out to help the very old," said Ralph.

25

Nader and his group discovered secrets that corporations tried to keep hidden. His discoveries shocked Americans. Corporate America was not happy about Ralph Nader. But that didn't bother him. He continued to work to change laws and to fight for the causes he believed in.

Some of these laws were passed around the time the Center was formed. They included the Freedom of Information Act of 1966, the Wholesome Meat Act of 1967, the Radiation Control for Health and Safety Act of 1968, the Coal Mine Health and Safety Act of 1969, and many others.

Students in the revolution

The Center brought students into the battle. It invited them to become junior investigators there. At least one hundred students applied for each job opening.

The late sixties was a period in America's history when all kinds of people began speaking up for equal rights and equal treatment under the law. Students, African-Americans, women, and antiwar protesters all took to the streets to protest injustices. Nader's crusade was part of all this.

The students who applied for work at the Center wanted — like Ralph — to make a better world. Each summer, students learned an important lesson about the power of the consumer. They learned that the system wasn't as hard to fight as they had thought. Students who used to fight for issues by simply accusing others now learned to use facts.

PIRGs

Nader saw his movement picking up speed. He started a second law firm called the Public Interest Research Group, or PIRG. In all, he would start nineteen such organizations.

This law firm's job was to build a network of PIRGs in other states and to increase the number of public-interest lawyers. The success of these groups showed Nader that citizen groups could work. He was setting an example that more and more people were following.

At the height of the Industrial Revolution, industry used children as cheap labor. This young girl and many thousands like her worked for pennies a day. Parents were horrified at the dangerous working conditions that their children often faced. But poor immigrants needed the money earned by their children. It was not until the middle class became alarmed by conditions for such children that laws were changed to regulate child labor.

Why had Americans waited so long to get involved in this way? How had innocent people let themselves be the victims of unfair and dishonest businesses? And why hadn't industry, advertising, and government been held responsible before the 1960s?

The roots of the problem

History answers some of these questions. As America grew, so did its problems. But America was not always the land of big business and advertising. Just over a century ago, most people lived in rural areas, making their own food, clothes, and tools. Or they traded with people who made them. The biggest factories were just small shops where articles were made by hand.

But this began to change in the 1860s. That's when America's Northern states went to war against the Southern states in the Civil War. The Civil War increased the demand for soldiers' uniforms. Until then, there were no set sizes for clothes. People had their clothes measured and made by hand. But the huge demand for uniforms created standard patterns and sizes. By the end of the war, an industry existed for ready-made men's clothing.

Twenty years later, the notion of clothes being ready-made was popular. The Industrial Revolution — using machines to make things that had been handmade — was in full swing. This was true in North America and Europe. Factories could produce goods cheaply, quickly, and be consistent as well.

It seemed to people that machines represented progress. People began to value articles made by machines. They looked down on items made by hand. More and more people moved away from the country to find jobs in city factories. The city dwellers then had little time or space to grow their own food or make their own clothes. So other factories were built to create inexpensive consumer goods in much larger numbers than had been possible before.

The makers of Cornea Restorers guaranteed a cure for many eye diseases. Phony cures like this were common in the days before consumers spoke up against companies that cheated and harmed them with useless, unsafe products.

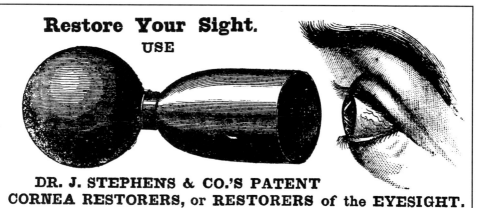

Restore Your Sight.
USE

DR. J. STEPHENS & CO.'S PATENT
CORNEA RESTORERS, or RESTORERS of the EYESIGHT.
They will Restore Impaired Sight, and Preserve it to the Latest Period of Life.
SPECTACLES RENDERED USELESS.

The most eminent Physicians, Oculists, Divines, and the most prominent men of our country, recommend the use of the CORNEA RESTORERS, for Presbyopia, or Far or Long Sightedness, or every person who wears spectacles from old age; Dimness of Vision, or Blurring; Overworked Eyes; Asthenopia, or Weak Eyes; Epiphora, or Watery Eyes: Pain in the Eyeball; Amaurosis, or Obscurity of Vision; Photophobia, or Intolerance of Light; Weakness of the Retina and Optic Nerve; Myodesopia, or Specks or Moving Bodies before the Eyes; Ophthalmia, or Inflammation of the Eye and Eyelids; Cataract Eyes; Hemiopia, or Partial Blindness; Sinking of the Eyeball; Strabismus, or Squinting, &c.

They can be used by any one with a certainty of success, and without the least fear of injury to the Eye. More than 5000 certificates of cures are exhibited at our office. Cure guaranteed in every case when applied according to the directions inclosed in each box, or the money will be refunded. Write for a Circular—sent gratis. Address

Dr. J. STEPHENS & CO., Oculists, at RUSHTON'S Family Drug Store, No. 10 Astor House, Broadway, New York. (P. O. Box 926). ☞ Dr. J. Stephens & Co. have invented and patented a MYOPIA, or CORNEA FLATTENER, for the cure of NEAR-SIGHTEDNESS, which has proved a great success. Write for a Circular.

Consumers become frustrated

Business wasn't as friendly as before. It became bigger and more impersonal. No longer were customers also the neighbors who lived nearby. Now, customers were people the factory owners had never met. And because there were so many more customers than before, there was a much greater demand for products. Factory owners were getting rich.

Some businessmen realized that they could make even more money if they were willing to be dishonest about their products. All they needed to do was use cheaper materials and charge the same prices as they had with higher-quality materials. Some of them even lied, saying that their products could do incredible things that no other product could do. People believed the promises and bought the products, thinking that the miracles would come true.

But some of the consumers became frustrated. What could they do about products that were poorly made or didn't do what they were supposed to?

There were no laws to protect the buyers. Besides, the businesses seemed too big and powerful for the small consumer to do anything about. A buyer might refuse to buy a particular product. But that wouldn't prevent the problem from happening again.

"The biggest problem in dealing with the government is the fact that 99% of the people don't want to be bothered."
Ralph Nader, quoted in Rolling Stone

Left: In 1883, Dr. Harvey W. Wiley became the first person to discover that the chemicals added to food to preserve them were harmful to humans.

Below: In 1906, President Theodore Roosevelt and the U.S. Congress passed the Pure Food and Drug Act. This happened after publication of The Jungle *frightened consumers. The act called for making meat-packing plants and other food factories cleaner.*

An early consumer advocate

Some people began to look into the quality of products that were available. One man did research on food additives (chemicals added to foods to keep them looking fresh). Dr. Harvey W. Wiley worked for the United States Department of Agriculture. Wiley wanted the U.S. government to set standards for keeping food pure. But government officials said they didn't want to interfere with the right of business to produce and sell goods without government restrictions.

So Wiley began to speak out publicly. He told audiences that some food was dangerous because it contained additives. And he proved his theory. He

Opposite: In 1967, Upton Sinclair and Nader witness the signing of the Wholesome Meat Act sixty-one years after The Jungle *first exposed the unsanitary conditions in meat-packing plants.*

fed a group of volunteers — known as the Poison Squad — food with additives. Soon some of them became ill. People were horrified. They began to protest the use of additives in food.

The Jungle

Then, in February 1906, a man named Upton Sinclair brought about a new panic. In his novel *The Jungle*, Sinclair described the filthy conditions in Chicago meat-packing plants. People were shocked to learn that the meat they ate was often mixed with dust, rodent hair, and even animal feces.

President Theodore Roosevelt sent agriculture officials to Chicago. He wanted them to check out Sinclair's story. They discovered that the novelist was telling the truth. The meat-packing plants *were* disgusting.

The public demanded a change, and Congress listened. Even though the meat industry protested loudly, Congress passed the Pure Food and Drug Act. It was supposed to guarantee that food and drugs would be carefully checked.

But while most people were happy with the new law, Wiley was not. This was because there was an important problem with the law. Congress had given in under pressure from angry businessmen. The law required any labels describing what was in the food to

be honest. But it did not *require* labels and it covered only meat transported across state lines. Wiley knew that this law wouldn't really protect people.

False claims

Wiley wanted to test the new law. So he sued a drug manufacturer who made a product that was called Brane-Fude. Manufacturer Robert Harper made big promises for his product. He said that Brane-Fude cured headaches. He also said that it nourished, or fed, the brain and would make a person healthier.

In February 1908, Harper was found guilty of violating the Pure Food and Drug Act. Wiley had proved that Harper was making false claims about his product. He was misleading the public. But there were still no rules about what a product should not contain.

During the Great Depression of the 1930s, many Americans were unemployed, poor, and hungry. Sights like this long line at a free soup kitchen were common.

Changes in America

More people complained about other products over the next few years. Then, in 1914, Congress created the Federal Trade Commission, or FTC. This agency was set up to guard against unfair business practices. The FTC also kept an eye on the advertising industry so it would not mislead the public.

World War I ended in 1918. In the years that followed, Americans wanted to forget the death and destruction of the war. America entered "the roaring twenties," a time when people wanted to stop thinking about their problems and have fun.

But in October 1929, the economy suffered a great crisis. Many people had bought shares, or small parts of companies. Suddenly those shares weren't worth much any more.

"If you saw them putting nine teaspoons of sugar into your soda, would you drink it?"
Ralph Nader, quoted in the Washington Post

After the hardships of the Great Depression and World War II, Americans went on the biggest shopping spree in history. They bought big, shiny cars and new wardrobes every year.

Factories and banks went out of business. Millions of people lost their jobs. Most people had little money to spend, so they were even more upset when something they bought didn't work. In some cases, products were even poisonous or deadly. Yet there was no law that required the labeling of ingredients on the package.

Then something awful happened which caused the government to pass a law requiring product labels. Over one hundred people died after taking a new medicine. There had been no list on the packages to tell doctors what was in the medicine, which contained poison.

So in June 1938, Congress passed the Food, Drug, and Cosmetic Act. The law said that all drugs would have to be tested to make sure they were safe and that they did what the makers of the products claimed they would do.

Postwar shopping spree

America entered World War II in December 1941. Again, money was scarce. There was a shortage of food, fuel, and many other goods. People could only buy a certain amount of everything, because of the war.

When the war ended in August 1945, Americans started buying. People who could afford it started buying new items, even if they didn't really need them.

Advertisers started looking at how people felt and thought. Why did they want all these new things? Advertisers realized they might be able to use this information in advertising.

So advertisements began to tell people that buying certain products would make them better somehow. The ads claimed that the products would make a person younger, smarter, or prettier. Of course, no product could do these things. But many people believed these claims.

In 1957, a man named Vance Packard published a book called *The Hidden Persuaders*. He showed the public how people were being convinced to buy things they didn't even need.

Consumers get angry

For the first time, a lot of consumers got upset about advertising. They felt cheated. People were also frustrated because many products were poorly made and broke easily. So they would end up buying new products. They didn't realize that the companies that made these products wanted them to break or wear out fast. That way, these companies could sell more products.

People also worried that garbage dumps would run out of room to hold all the junk they threw away. The more industry produced, the more waste products were created.

Top: In 1962, Dr. Frances Kelsey urges the U.S. Senate to ban thalidomide.

Bottom: Freddie Astbury, age 13, whose birth defects resulted from thalidomide. The drug crippled 432 children.

No one to turn to

There didn't seem to be anyone who cared about the problems of the ordinary consumer. No one was stopping these companies from cheating the public. There was talk, but not much action.

There were a few cases of companies getting caught, however. The company that made a drug called thalidomide was an example. Thalidomide caused hundreds of severe birth defects in babies born to European women in 1962. Babies of women who had taken the drug were often born without arms or legs or both. Then an American doctor, Frances Kelsey, of the Food and Drug Administration, uncovered the facts. Her investigation brought a ban on the use of thalidomide in Europe. It also kept the manufacturer from selling the drug in the United States.

The antitrust laws were another example. Senator Estes Kefauver uncovered a group of dishonest businesses that set prices much too high and then tried to prevent any other company from selling similar products. But these were isolated cases. There was still no organized attack against unsafe products or dishonest business practices.

It was time for someone to step forward and speak out for consumers. In 1966, with Nader's exposure of General Motors and the Corvair, that someone had arrived. Ralph Nader became the voice for consumers. And he and his Raiders have been doing tough investigations since that time.

Lots of sacrifices

But to do what he has done, Nader has had to give up things most people enjoy. He decided never to marry or have children. He called this a "cruel choice," but he knew that his late hours would make it difficult to have a family.

Ralph has always lived very simply. For many years he lived in one room in a boarding house. Then, in the 1980s, he moved into an inexpensive apartment in the same neighborhood.

He doesn't own a television, and he hardly ever drives a car. He used to own just a few plain suits and two pairs of black shoes. But now he dresses up a little more, although not too expensively.

Nader makes hundreds of thousands of dollars from his lectures and appearances. But he puts most of that money back into running the Center. He doesn't date or go out with friends. His only treat to himself is that he will eat two desserts when he gets a chance. He says that he can live on $11,000 a year. With today's high rents and food costs, that is not a lot of money to live on!

Nader lives simply so he can use his time and energy to make the world a

SURGEON GENERAL'S WARNING: Quitting Smoking Now Greatly Reduces Serious Risks to Your Health.

SURGEON GENERAL'S WARNING: Cigarette Smoke Contains Carbon Monoxide.

SURGEON GENERAL'S WARNING: Smoking By Pregnant Women May Result in Fetal Injury, Premature Birth, And Low Birth Weight.

SURGEON GENERAL'S WARNING: Smoking Causes Lung Cancer, Heart Disease, Emphysema, And May Complicate Pregnancy.

Pressure from consumer groups and doctors resulted in health warnings on American cigarette packages. Cigarette companies fought the requirement, fearing that consumers would reject their product. Other rulings prohibit cigarette commercials on television or radio.

*Edward M. Swartz,
author of* Toys That
Kill, *displayed
dangerous toys before
the U.S. Senate
Commerce Committee
in 1971.*

better place. He doesn't want to buy a lot of useless junk. In fact, he even feels upset when people who work for him buy new cars or other products.

Some consumers resent Ralph

Not everyone thinks Ralph Nader is the greatest. This is because while he fights for consumer rights, he also asks that consumers moderate their behavior. He wants people to think before they buy. If it's not necessary, don't buy it. If it might harm someone, don't buy it.

Some consumers resent his attitude about buying things. What's wrong, they ask, with buying a VCR or a hot dog if that's what you feel like buying?

Business leaders resent him, too

Nader also annoys some people in business. They say nobody forces people to buy products they don't want. They only make what the public wants. If a product is useless or dangerous, they say, people shouldn't buy it.

But Nader says that people often find out how bad the product is only after their money has been spent. And maybe they have already been hurt by the product. Consumers want businesses to be honest. Why should the buyer always have to suspect that the product might be poorly made?

It is not lazy consumers that create so much tragedy and waste, Nader says. Rather, it's businesses that encourage secrecy and waste. Nader feels that the careless or greedy businesses who cause the problems should take the blame, not the consumers.

Ralph has exposed many harmful and unfair business practices. He has shown how some businesses use dangerous materials or materials that have been banned. And he has shown how some companies label products unclearly just to confuse the consumer.

No one with something to hide likes to be investigated by Ralph. Whether they are illegally releasing chemicals into rivers or selling unclean food, the name Ralph Nader makes them very nervous.

"I wasn't anti-business then, and I'm not anti-business now. I'm just pro-people."
Ralph Nader, quoted
in Richard Curtis'
Ralph Nader's Crusade

41

Opposite: Ralph Nader criticized the Food and Drug Administration in 1988 for trying to kill a rule that makes fruit juice companies reveal the amount of real juice in their products. New York State attorney general Robert Abrams looks on.

Raiders meet his standards

It isn't always easy for the Raiders to follow the example of a man like Nader. For one thing, he is almost never at the Center. And usually he doesn't tell people where he is. He is often traveling, making speeches about consumer advocacy. If a problem comes up, his staff has to solve it on their own.

And when Ralph is there, he seems uncomfortable with everybody. Instead of talking with his staff, he prefers reading or writing all day. It seems strange that a man so concerned with the public could be so shy.

One Raider told Ralph that the staff wanted Ralph to be more of a friend and guide to them. Nader was baffled. They had the freedom to work on whatever they wanted. Why, he asked, would they want time with him?

Working for Ralph Nader

People who work for Ralph know about the job before they accept it. They also know that to work for Ralph is to work all the time. Sometimes, Nader will call his workers in the middle of the night. If the telephone rings late, they just answer, "Hello, Ralph."

He manages his staff with one simple principle: He does not ask them to do anything that he himself will not do. But he expects a good deal of himself, so he

Rulings now require warning labels like the one below. Before consumer advocates like Nader demanded such labels on packages, people were often injured or killed using products improperly.

Caution: Do not give to children under 12 years of age or use for more than 10 days unless directed by a physician. **WARNINGS: AS WITH ANY DRUG, IF YOU ARE PREGNANT OR NURSING A BABY, SEEK THE ADVICE OF A HEALTH PROFESSIONAL BEFORE USING THIS PRODUCT. KEEP THIS AND ALL DRUGS OUT OF REACH OF CHILDREN. IN CASE OF ACCIDENTAL OVERDOSE SEEK PROFESSIONAL ASSISTANCE OR CONTACT A POISON CONTROL CENTER IMMEDIATELY.**

expects a good deal of his workers, too. He often goes without sleep and food. He never takes vacations and usually works on weekends.

Even though this is a tough example to live up to, Ralph's workers also take their work seriously. While they might take a Saturday off to be with their families, that doesn't happen often.

"Dear Ralph Nader . . . "

Although Ralph has some critics, most people believe in him. Every day, the Center receives hundreds of letters. Ordinary people complain about products or companies and ask that Nader investigate them.

Nader's consumer groups study the letters. Often they can spot troubling trends and dangerous products because of what people are writing. Many of the letter writers are angry. Some people who write Nader even want to join one of his organizations.

Ralph's sister, Claire Nader, is an anthropologist. An anthropologist is someone who studies the way people behave and get along together. She is interested in the effects of stress on consumers. She wrote a book about the difficulty consumers have in getting help when they have been treated unfairly. Part of the book included letters written to her brother. The book is called *No*

Access to Law: Alternatives to the American Judicial System.

The letters show people's frustration — and how people believe in Nader and hope he can change the way things are. "Oh, Mr. Nader," writes one person. "They cheat like the devil himself — all of them. How many times have I bought boiled ham in a cellophane wrapping, only to find when I lifted up the top two slices, the rest was bits and pieces heavily laced with fat."

"Dear Ralph Nader," another person writes. "I was so glad to read you are investigating the medical profession. It would be impossible for me to describe what I've undergone for 8 years due to a wrong medical diagnosis, and a sloppy operation, performed by an unqualified surgeon. I've lost piles of money. . . . So this terrible operation, which I didn't need in the first place, has cost me a normal life, and exposed to me the largest group of racketeers in existence — the doctors."

"Dear Mr. Nader," another letter reads. "The things I could tell you about [a state institution for people who are retarded] would make your hair stand straight up. They brought [my son] out to us with two swollen black eyes . . . [and] with cigarette burns on the bottoms of his feet. Please investigate and make a loud noise about the whole thing."

"One day we walked into a little food mart and got a popsicle and my friend Tom said his tasted funny. So I said lets get your money back. So we went back and said we wished to get our money back or we would write to Ralph Nader. So he said go ahead. So we are writing you. Mike."

From letter to Nader, quoted in Robert Buckhorn's Nader, the People's Lawyer

Learning to think like Nader

Just from these few letters, it is plain to Ralph Nader that all different kinds of consumers are victims. Many suffer because of dishonest businesses and dangerous products.

Nader can't write back to each person who writes him. But every letter makes him more determined to stop consumers from being taken advantage of. Nader and his organizations investigate many of the activities that make people suffer. By checking out these complaints, he hopes he can make businesses and government take responsibility for their mistakes and correct them.

Ralph remembers how his mother encouraged him to stop complaining about a problem and do something about it. He developed a way of looking at things that taught him to question poorly and dangerously designed products. He questions everything.

"Take, for instance, the front bumper of an automobile," he tells consumers in just one case. "Nearly every day most people casually look at car bumpers. Their view usually stops there. A few moments of consumer education would open the following sequence:

"Bumpers are supposed to protect automobiles from minor damage in minor collisions. For many years, however, bumper design has been largely ornamental. Much needless damage has resulted when cars bumped or crashed at two, three, five or eight miles an hour. Such damage costs motorists over one billion dollars a year. . . . Why did the auto companies design such bumpers? Could it be the companies profited by faulty design and covered their actions by promoting the [looks] of egg-shell bumpers?"

The investigations

Ralph's fight to expose faulty car production is what made him famous. Yet he has been responsible for far more than changes in car design. These are some of the most famous reports written by Nader and his Raiders:

• *The Chemical Feast*, an investigation

Poisonous chemicals spew from a smokestack in Pennsylvania and return to earth in the form of acid rain, killing forests and wildlife, even corroding cars and buildings.

Because of many investigations by Nader and other public citizens, nursing homes now regulate themselves more strictly and must meet standards for cleanliness and safety.

into the Food and Drug Administration's lazy enforcement of laws banning certain additives in food;

• *The Vanishing Air*, a report on the shocking truth about air pollution, and how industries ignore laws designed to stop them from sending deadly chemicals into the air, water, and soil;

• *Old Age: The Last Segregation*, about the disgusting and tragic conditions in homes for the elderly;

• *Bitter Wages: Disease and Injury on the Job*, which shows how employers often ignore dangerous, even deadly, working conditions. They also ignore the suffering of workers injured because of dangerous work places.

Of course, there are many other reports. All expose important problems that deal with consumer issues. The reports let the public know about these problems. But then what happens? The media publish the details of the terrible conditions, and the public then demands that the situation be changed.

But Nader doesn't stick around to see that the wrong turns right. He and his Raiders are already looking into new problems. Some of Nader's critics think he should continue working on a problem until it is solved. But he says there are far too many problems for him to spend too much time on each one.

Some of the problems he has uncovered deal with land use, pollution, food and drug additives, unsafe toys, antitrust laws, unsafe x-ray exposure, housing abuses, banking power, medical services, the U.S. Congress, false advertising, women's issues, insurance fraud, lethal pesticides, and much more.

Ralph's method of exposing these wrongs does work. It gets attention and raises the awareness of the public.

Setting a trend

Nader knew that he alone could not make these changes. He knew that other people must follow his example and get involved. They formed hundreds of consumer organizations that fight for people's rights. They pressure lawmakers to vote on issues that are important to them. And often, they see that new laws are passed.

But even with new laws, some unsafe products and practices still exist.

Pollution: a consumer issue

Perhaps one of the worst problems of all is pollution of the environment. Ralph and his Raiders have worked hard on this issue. The public breathes the foul air and drinks the poisoned water that industries create. So Nader considers pollution a consumer issue.

Some business leaders claim they don't support pollution control and safety research because it would cost the consumer too much. But Ralph doesn't believe that. He has dedicated his life to exposing these claims as myths. Industry tells these lies to hide wasteful, dangerous practices, he says.

Industries, Nader and many others note, save money when they just dump their toxic waste into rivers and lakes instead of storing it in safe containers. And they save money by letting poisonous gas belch from their smokestacks into the air, instead of putting in expensive pollution-control equipment to protect the environment.

One of the most dangerous polluters, Nader says, is the nuclear industry. It is very careless about the waste from the nuclear power plants. This waste is known to cause cancer in humans. But Nader has discovered that the people who own and manage nuclear plants don't want to admit that the public could be in danger.

Ralph believes it is the duty of the industry that produces toxic wastes to pay the cleanup bills. Even though it is expensive, Nader doesn't think business should put expense ahead of public health and safety.

The cooling towers of the Three Mile Island nuclear power plant. This plant is the site of the worst nuclear accident in U.S. history.

Quality of life

It is impossible to guess the number of lives that have been saved or made better because of Ralph Nader's career as a consumer advocate. But it is possible to see the kinds of improvements that have been made because of his hard work.

Badly made cars are now recalled by their makers and safety defects are repaired. Cars now have standard safety features, like seat belts, safety glass, and sometimes even air bags.

Hot dogs used to be 30 percent fat — even though most manufacturers didn't

"Open your window and take a deep breath. You'll feel lousy."
A print advertisement of the 1960s, protesting air pollution, quoted in Richard Curtis' Ralph Nader's Crusade

51

tell the buyers. But now hot dogs can't contain more than 15 percent fat. Additives, other ingredients, and nutritional content in food must appear on the package label.

Cigarette packages must carry health warnings. Cigarette commercials are banned from television. Airplanes, restaurants, and public buildings have nonsmoking sections.

Toys that have injured children have been removed from stores. Fabrics used to make children's pajamas must be made nonflammable.

Workers must now have physical protection from dangerous chemicals and poisons. Advertising may not make false claims about a product.

Ralph Nader once called hot dogs "America's most dangerous unguided missiles" because they were 30 percent fat. Today, hot dogs may have 15 percent fat at most. Meat packers must list ingredients, including chemical preservatives, on the package.

Quieter years

Since 1975, Ralph Nader has been less outspoken. He still lectures, but not as much. He used to speak to about 150 audiences a year. Now that number is closer to thirty.

In 1986, Ralph's older brother, Shafik, died of cancer. For the first time in over twenty years, Ralph stopped working. He went to stay with his parents at their home in Winsted, Connecticut. When he returned to work, his co-workers thought he seemed quieter than usual.

Ralph had been doing a lot of thinking while he was gone. He still cared about making products safer. But he decided to put his energy into a few projects, instead of trying to tackle every problem at once.

And then he became ill. He caught the disease called Bell's palsy. It froze the right side of his face and made it hard for him to talk, eat, or even smile. Doctors told Ralph that he had to stop working so hard. Gradually, he recovered until his face twitched only a bit.

"I have a very stable set of purposes and convictions. I know it is going to be a rocky road so I am not ruffled very easily. I am sort of programmed to anticipate all these things, and I try to do what I can to prepare myself. I don't get all clutched up or nervous if things go wrong. I have an inner consistency that carries me through."

Ralph Nader, quoted in Robert Buckhorn's Nader, the People's Lawyer

Changes in Winsted

While he was in Winsted, Ralph noticed menacing changes in his hometown. He was worried about its future. He noticed that a rich land developer had bought almost a million dollars' worth of beautiful, wooded land in Winsted. This man wanted to tear down his own house,

"There has been concern among a lot of consumer people that Ralph was overextending himself."

A member of the Carter administration, formerly a consumer advocate, quoted in U.S. News & World Report

53

a historically important building dating back to the American Revolution. The developer said it was not useful.

Also, a giant mall was being built just outside of town. Ralph was worried that traffic and ugliness were about to disrupt his hometown. But worse than that, nobody seemed to care!

After Shafik's death, Ralph felt even more attached to his hometown. He wanted to keep the town as beautiful as it had been when he was a child. So he and his sister Claire began to organize the people of Winsted to protest the development. They hired a citizen activist who helped the townspeople circulate petitions. People put pressure on the local government to stop the development. They hired a lawyer to

The main street of Winsted, Connecticut, where Ralph Nader lived as a boy.

fight the case in local courts. Ralph was helping his own former neighbors fight for their rights.

Back in the national eye

In 1988, Ralph Nader suddenly returned to the national scene. He helped people in California pass a law by referendum — by popular vote. The referendum made automobile insurance companies lower what they charged people.

Until the referendum, Californians paid the highest car insurance rates in the country. Sometimes they paid thousands of dollars more than people in other parts of the country — for the exact same kind of insurance!

Ralph realized that people could come together and create a public uprising out of the issue. He gave talks. Fighting against him were insurance companies that spent $70 million to convince the voters to vote against the proposal. A group called Voter Revolt formed. This group spent only $2 million. But it was able to rally the voters to pass the law lowering insurance rates.

A poll taken later showed that two-thirds of California voters would have voted to pass the proposal, Proposition 103, just because Ralph Nader's name was associated with the cause. Once again, Nader was in the middle of the battle for fairness and honesty.

To prevent land development in Winsted, Claire Nader joined forces with her famous brother.

"My father taught me a long time ago that the highest thing after attaining a measure of progress or success is to be able to endure it. That is what I always counsel the students. Don't let that ego get in your way. Don't start getting a swollen head. Keep your eye on the objective and work harder, and harder, and harder."

Ralph Nader, quoted in Robert Buckhorn's Nader, the People's Lawyer

From apples to Congress

Nader worked hard in 1988 on several other important causes. He worked to stop apple farmers from using Alar, a chemical pesticide, on their orchards. The Food and Drug Administration had discovered that Alar caused a high rate of cancer in children. Now there is a government ban on the use of Alar by apple farmers.

Ralph also fought Congress when it wanted to give each member of the House and Senate a large pay raise. Again, Ralph sensed the citizens' anger at the members of Congress for trying to give themselves large raises when the economy was in such bad shape. That year, Congress listened to Nader and the public and didn't give itself a raise. But the next year there were raises for all the senators and representatives.

The future through Ralph's eyes

Nader believes very strongly that people should stand up and fight to protect themselves from unfair business practices and greedy and inefficient government officials. He wants ordinary citizens to try to make life better for the whole community rather than wait for their government to fix the problems. He also believes that group action can help solve consumer problems. His views on the way people should attack the

"Patriotism begins at home. Love of country in fact is inseparable from citizen action to make the country more lovable. This means working to end poverty, discrimination, corruption, greed and other conditions that weaken the promise and potential of America."

Ralph Nader, Life, July 1971

problems that affect them has changed the way people view themselves, businesses, and the government.

"Consumers should be assertive enough to turn their economy into a buyer's market," Nader said. In other words, they should make the decisions about what is sold, rather than allow big business to tell them what to do.

Why we need Ralph Nader

Ralph Nader has helped make major changes in the way business and government operate. But he probably will be remembered more for teaching people how to fight to change things.

He has changed the way consumers look at what they buy. He has showed Americans that it is right to fight dishonest businesses. He has shown people how to protest and get results. Ralph has also shown that the government is not set up to fight for consumers' rights.

Today, the public is more ready to make demands. Americans are no longer willing to sit back while careless businesses damage people's lives. Companies and politicians alike know they will have to answer to a concerned and questioning public.

"It's your system," Nader has said. "It's up to you to make it work better."

Ralph has been a good teacher — so

"How do you get people to become serious about deciding things for themselves instead of letting other people decide things for them?"
Ralph Nader, quoted in
Rolling Stone

"I think he started something that has become much larger than he is. While he is still an important part of it, the consumer movement has in fact grown larger than Ralph."
Carole Tucker Foreman,
assistant secretary of
agriculture for the Carter
administration, quoted in
U.S. News & World Report

good that people don't need him as much as when he first began his work. Since he started the consumer revolution, many of his ideas have been accepted as common wisdom. He has become a symbol to ordinary citizens who now know that they can bring about important changes for themselves and for others. He stands for turning wrongs into rights. He has convinced America that people count.

Opposite: Many of the revolutionary things Ralph Nader believed as an early consumer advocate are common wisdom now. People are now more aware of food additives and the safety of their homes, cars, and work places.

To find out more . . .

Organizations

The groups listed below can give you more information about consumer rights, about laws designed to protect the consumer, about environmental concerns of interest to the consumer, and about mismanagement in government. Write to them if you would like to know more about issues of interest to you. When you write, be sure to tell them exactly what you would like to know. Also include your name, address, and age.

Americans for Democratic Action
1511 K Street NW, Suite 941
Washington, DC 20005

Center for the Study of Responsive Law
P.O. Box 19367
Washington, DC 20036

Citizens Against Government Waste
1511 K Street NW, Suite 643
Washington, DC 20005

Consumer Education and Protective Association International
6048 Ogontz Avenue
Philadelphia, PA 19141

Public Citizen
P.O. Box 19404
Washington, DC 20036

Public Information Center
U.S. Environmental Protection Agency (EPA)
401 M Street SW
Washington, DC 20460

For U.S. government pamphlets for consumers . . .
Consumer Information Center
Pueblo, CO 81009

For questions about consumer protection, food, drugs, cosmetics, and electronics . . .
Food and Drug Administration
Office of Consumer Affairs
5600 Fishers Lane, Room 16-63
Rockville, MD 20857

Books

The following books can help you learn more about some of the topics discussed in this book. Check your library or bookstore to see if they have these books or can order them for you.

Conservation. Richard Gates (Childrens Press)
Conservation and Pollution. Laurence Santrey (Troll)
Jacques Cousteau: Free Flight Undersea. Paul Westman (Dillon)
Junk Food — What It Is; What It Does. Judith S. Seixas (Greenwillow)
Our Living Planet. Paula Hogan (Gareth Stevens)
Pollution and Conservation. David Lambert (Franklin Watts)
Rachel Carson: Pioneer of Ecology. Ted Lewin (Penguin)
Save the Earth! An Ecology Handbook for Kids. Betty Miles (Knopf)
Silent Spring. Rachel Carson (Houghton Mifflin)

List of new words

additives
> Substances added to food to improve taste and shelf life. Many additives are unnecessary and unsafe for humans.

antitrust
> A term that describes laws regulating businesses so that they will not have an unfair advantage in the marketplace.

consumer

A person who buys a product or service.

consumer advocate

A person, like Ralph Nader, who fights for consumers, or argues for the cause of consumers.

corporation

A type of organization formed by a group of people. A typical corporation is usually a business run by its managers or owners.

Corvair

A sports car designed and produced by General Motors from 1959 to 1969. This car was the center of Nader's argument that American carmakers cared more about sporty looks and making money than about consumer safety.

DDT

A clear insecticide that can harm humans and animals when swallowed or absorbed by the skin. DDT was once used to spray crops and trees against insect damage.

fraud

A dishonest scheme used to make money unfairly. Some advertisers make fraudulent claims about their products in order to boost sales and make more money.

harass

To bother or annoy someone in order to change that person's mind or influence that person in some other way.

Industrial Revolution

The period from the late 1700s through the early 1900s. During this time, the economy shifted from agriculture to industry. Large numbers of products were made in factories to sell worldwide rather than by hand to sell locally.

occupational safety
Safety on the job. Employers must tell all workers about any dangerous chemicals or machinery in the work place. They must also protect them from these hazards.

public citizen
A term used by Nader to describe a resident who actively takes part in the decisions of his or her community. The public citizen makes sure that government and business serve the interests of the public.

public-interest issues
Issues that affect the life, health, and well-being of the public. For example, environmental pollution and dangerous cars, toys, and other products are matters of public interest.

thalidomide
A sedative drug that caused severe birth defects when used by pregnant women. This harmful drug is no longer sold.

toxic waste
Any poisonous by-product of industrial or nuclear production (whether liquid, solid, or gas). The release of toxic waste into the environment can cause death and disease in living things.

Important dates

1865   The American Civil War increases demand for uniforms. Men's ready-made clothing industry is created.

1880s The Industrial Revolution increases production of consumer goods.

1883   Dr. Harvey W. Wiley notices chemical additives in food and argues unsuccessfully for a pure food law.

1890s	Wiley speaks out publicly for removal of impurities and additives from food.
1900- 1914	Reform movements, including the consumer movement, become popular in the United States. This period is called the Progressive Era.
1902	Wiley conducts experiment with food additives to see their effect on human health. He publishes "The Poison Squad."
1906	**February** — Upton Sinclair publishes *The Jungle*. This book describes the filthy and disgusting conditions in many meat-packing plants. **June** — Public outrage over *The Jungle* moves Congress to pass Pure Food and Drug Act. But this law does not list impurities to be banned.
1908	**February** — Robert N. Harper becomes the first person convicted of violating Pure Food and Drug Act; he misleads the public about his product, Brane-Fude.
1912	The Association of Advertising Clubs of America founds the Better Business Bureau to devise a code of business ethics and discourage advertising dishonesty. Nathra and Rose Nader move from their native Lebanon to rural Winsted, Connecticut, with their son, Shafik.
1914	The Federal Trade Commission is formed to ensure fair competition among businesses and to monitor the advertising industry.
1929	**October** — The Great Depression begins: the New York Stock Exchange crashes; factories and banks fail; eventually millions are out of work.
1930	Wiley, "Father of the Pure Food Law," dies at 85.

1934   **February 27** — Ralph Nader is born to Nathra and Rose Nader.

1938   **June 25** — Despite business opposition, the Food, Drug, and Cosmetic Act passes suddenly because of 107 deaths resulting from a harmful drug.

1941   **December 7** — America enters World War II. Food, fuel, and consumer goods become scarce as industry produces military equipment.

1945   **August 14** — World War II ends. Americans begin era of huge consumer spending to make up for war shortages. Unprecedented numbers of children are born in postwar rebuilding. Buying becomes America's pastime.

1951   Ralph Nader enters Princeton University.

1952   *Consumer Reports* subscriptions reach one-half million.

1953   The Flammable Fabrics Act passes. It requires that all children's pajamas be made of material that does not easily catch fire.

1955   Ralph Nader enters Harvard Law School.

1957   Vance Packard's book *The Hidden Persuaders* shows how the advertising industry uses psychological techniques to get consumers to buy products.

1958   Nader's first published article, "American Cars: Designed for Death," appears in the *Harvard Law School Record*.

1959   General Motors puts dangerous Corvair car on the market without properly testing it for safety.

1960	Senator John F. Kennedy is elected president and promises to become the consumers' lobbyist.
1961	Dr. Frances Kelsey finds that the drug thalidomide causes severe birth defects. The drug is outlawed in Europe and prevented from being sold in the United States.
1964	Nader moves to Washington, D.C., to work for Daniel Patrick Moynihan at the U.S. Department of Labor. He soon leaves department to write full-time.
1965	**November** — Nader publishes *Unsafe at Any Speed*. This book exposes fatal design of some automobiles and demands that automakers pay attention to safety. General Motors hires detectives to investigate Nader's private life, hoping to damage his public image.
1966	**February** — Nader testifies before Congress on automobile safety. **March** — James Roche, chairman of General Motors, publicly apologizes to Nader for the illegal investigation of his private life. **June** — Nader sues General Motors for invasion of privacy, winning a $425,000 settlement.
1969	**May** — Nader establishes Center for the Study of Responsive Law (CSRL) in Washington, D.C., to fight for the public interest.
1970	Nader establishes the Public Interest Research Group (PIRG), a law firm resulting in a network of student organizations fighting for local issues.
1971	Ralph Nader is named to the Gallup Poll's "Most Admired Men" list.

1974   Nader edits CSRL's *Comprehensive Manual for Citizen Access to Federal Agencies.*

1976   Ralph Nader is placed on the ballot in Massachusetts as a presidential candidate. He demands that his name be removed, calls for a halt to export of hazardous products to other countries, and calls nuclear energy a "menace."

1977   Nader accuses Joan Claybrook, president of Public Citizen, Inc., of betraying consumers by supporting a Carter administration decision to allow automakers six years to install air bags in cars.

1978   Nader fights in Congress to establish a Consumer Protection Agency. His effort fails.

1981   Nader proclaims the Reagan administration to be "my next Corvair."

1986   Nader's brother, Shafik, dies of cancer at his home in Winsted, Connecticut.
Nader gets Bell's palsy and must limit his schedule.
Ralph and Claire Nader hire Ellen Thomas, a citizen activist, to save Winsted from overdevelopment.

1988   Nader works to stop apple farmers from using Alar on their crops. Public outcry results when the FDA states that this pesticide causes cancer in children.

1989   Nader tells Congress that its members should not receive pay raises. While at first he persuades Congress, members later vote themselves raises. Nader begins a fight to reverse that decision.

Index